REVOLUTION FARM

Inspired by George Orwell's Animal Farm

By James Kenworth

Published by Playdead Press 2022

© James Kenworth 2022

James Kenworth has asserted his rights under the Copyright, Design and Patents Act, 1988, to be identified as the authors of this work.

A CIP catalogue record for this book is available from the British Library.

ISBN 978-1-910067-98-7

Caution
All rights whatsoever in this play are strictly reserved and application for performance should be sought through the author before rehearsals begin. No performance may be given unless a license has been obtained.

This book is sold subject to the condition that it shall not by way of trade or otherwise, be lent, resold, hired out, or otherwise circulated without the publisher's prior consent in any form of binding or cover other than that in which it is published and without a similar condition including this condition being imposed on the subsequent purchaser.

Playdead Press
www.playdeadpress.com

Revolution Farm was first performed at Newham City Farm, Beckton on 19th August, 2014.

MAIN CAST

Old Boy	The Company
Daddy Love	Nicola Alexis
Hero	Samuel Caseley
Smoothy	Andreas Angelis
Warrior	Kevin Kinson
Lil' Monster	Katie Arnstein

YOUNG ACTORS

Pigeonhead	Zacchaeus Joseph
Rooster	Jaylan Joseph
Goatface	Michael Jnr Roberts
Black Sheep	Tyrone Ferguson
Donkeykick	Brandon Guioro
Ducklife	Abubacar Samba Bali
Red Hen	Shania Roberts
Dogs/Hens	Aisha Creary
	Georgina Shidah

PRODUCTION TEAM

Playwright	James Kenworth
Director	James Martin Charlton
Associate Producer	Stella Odunlami
Set & Costume Designer	Ian Teague
Production Manager	Ciaran Cunningham
Movement	Omar Okai
Assistant Director	Connor Abbott
Stage Manager	Katie Thackery
Production Assistant	Abel Diaz
Press Relations	Kevin Wilson
Photography & Graphic Design	Prodeepta Das
Young People's Mentors	Ailsa McPhee
	Susannah Austin

Writer's note

In 2010, Community Link's co-founder Kevin Jenkins, arranged for me to be a Writer-in-Residence at the Farm, to utilize the farm as a creative stimulus and encourage visitors, especially families and young people, to engage in a series of creative writing exercises designed to celebrate the farm and its work.

By 2014 the Farm had invested in a new performance space in the shape of a freshly built Play Barn, an open-sided oak-framed barn with a high roof. Kevin had invited me down to take a look at it with a view to performing a play on the Farm. The Barn was bigger and roomier than I expected and clearly had potential as an interesting performance space. But it wasn't just the Play Barn that the Farm had invested in. There was a new outdoor covered learning space too. And a play area complete with ride-on toys. Looking around at the cows, horses, sheep, and in particular, Alfie, the Berkshire pig, who appeared to elevate wallowing in mud to an art form, there was only one story that came to mind that would provide a perfect symbiosis between site and subject matter...Orwell's *Animal Farm.*

Newham City Farm sits in the shadows of Canary Wharf, home to many of the world's banks and is a symbol of global wealth and power. It was born out of Margaret Thatcher's free-market revolution and a trickle-down economics theory that promised wealth would eventually trickle down to everyone else, a claim many living in East London would perhaps robustly reject.

The subversive potential of the farm was irresistible. I would write a contemporary, urban version of Orwell's classic tale of greed and exploitation, with one of the UK's main financial centres as its backdrop. The aim was to take Orwell's satire on greed and corruption and give it a distinct whiff of Austerity Britain.

The researching and writing of *Revolution Farm* had been influenced by popular social upheavals such as the London Riots of 2011, especially the question of whether the police had lost control during the riots, as was suggested by several media commentators at the time. What if the London Riots had not been stopped, just what would a revolution by lawless young people look like?

The use of urban demotic speech together with the cast dressed in hoodies and trackies gave the play an unmistakable contemporary relevance, but you can achieve this effect just as well in a conventional theatre auditoria. What I think was unique and original about *Revolution Farm* was its setting and the Farm's surrounding environs that gave the production a genuinely troubling and disconcerting edge. This was theatre stripped away of all its usual niceties, no seats, no curtains, no lights, no ice creams. All that was required was a willing suspension of disbelief that an inner-city farm could be the battleground for a violent overthrow of power and privilege, and that its message of revolution might be closer to home than we think.

James Kenworth, 2021

The *Revolution Farm* company would like to thank the following for their generous help and support:

Our Activity Partners, **Theatre Royal Stratford East** and **Stratford Circus**, and in particular, Theatre Royal's Jan Sharkey-Dodds, Head of Young People's Work, and Serena B Robbins, Project Manager, Young People's Work.

Sam Clarke, Associate AHT / Pupil Premium / Head of Drama, **The Royal Docks Community School.**

Matthew Cornet, Class Teacher, **Gallions Primary School.**

Andrea Downer, Subject Leader for Drama, **Kingsford Community School.**

Mark Townsend, Area Manager, **Gainsborough Learning Centre.**

An especial thank you to Theresa, Anna, Stephanie and all the staff at **Newham City Farm** who have made the *Revolution Farm* company feel at home on the Farm, and to the animals themselves who have managed with the presence of noisy thespians in their midst very well.

Revolution Farm is supported by Royal Docks Trust/London Borough of Newham Main Programme Funding 2014/15.

Revolution Farm is supported using public funding by the National Lottery through Arts Council England.

Like Eastlea Community School's 2012 production of *When Chaplin Met Gandhi,* **Revolution Farm** is a unique collaboration between professional theatre artists and young people in Newham, involving a professional writer, director, designer and actors working alongside students from Newham schools and young actors from local youth groups/theatres.

As one of the most deprived parts of the UK, and traditionally a 'cold spot' for the arts, where engagement and participation in this sector, particularly among young people, is very low, Newham has recently seen a resurgence in the arts, especially Newham Mayor's ground breaking *Every Child A Musician* and *Every Child A Theatregoer* programmes.

By having Newham's school pupils as active participants, as actors, in **Revolution Farm**, we hope this will help strengthen and sustain the resurgence of interest in the arts in Newham, as well as introducing a whole new young generation to the work of George Orwell.

Special permission has been given by AM Heath on behalf of the George Orwell Estate for the production at Newham City Farm.

ANIMAL FARM by George Orwell published by Penguin Modern Classics.

Main Cast and Crew Biographies

James Kenworth | *Writer*
James Kenworth is a playwright and academic. His plays include *Johnny Song* (Warehouse Theatre, Croydon), *Gob* (King's Head Theatre, Pleasance Dome Edinburgh, Courtyard Theatre), *Polar Bears* (Iron Belly Edinburgh), *Everybody's World* (London tour), *Mere Yadhee* (London tour). He has written a series of localist-based, East End plays utilizing non-traditional and unconventional theatre spaces in the community, collectively known as 'The Newham Plays'. *When Chaplin Met Gandhi* (Kingsley Hall, Bow), *Revolution Farm* (Newham City Farm, Beckton), *A Splotch of Red: Keir Hardie in West Ham* (Community Links, Canning Town; Newham Libraries) and *Alice in Canning Town* (Arc in the Park, Canning Town). All four Newham plays have been published. He has lectured at UEL and is Lecturer in Media Narrative at Middlesex University.

James Martin Charlton | *Director*
James Martin Charlton is a dramatist, director and academic. His plays include *Fat Souls*, *Coming Up* (Warehouse Theatre, Croydon), *ecstasy + Grace* (Finborough), *Desires of Frankenstein* (Open Air, Regents Park), *The World & his Wife*, *I Really Must be Getting Off* (White Bear), *Coward* (Just Some Theatre Co., published by Playdead Press) and two short pieces for The Miniaturists, *Fellow Creature* and *Battis Boy* (Arcola Theatre). He has directed a number of contemporary plays, including *Gob, Bumps* (King's Head), *Plastic Zion, Leonardo's Ring, Virginia Plane, Amphibious Babies* (White Bear), *Histrionics* (Underbelly, Edinburgh), *Johnny Song* (Warehouse, Croydon). He directed *Tommy* and *A Twist of Oliver* at Maidstone Prison with casts of inmates and staff. He

has written and directed two short films, *Apeth* and *Academic*. He wrote screenplays for the shorts *Emotional Tribunal* and *Best Shot*. He has lectured at UEL and Birkbeck and is currently Senior Lecturer in Scriptwriting and Director of Programmes for Media Arts at Middlesex University.

Stella Odunlami | *Associate Producer*
Stella Odunlami is a Director and Artist. Credits as a Director include *Dies Irae* (Hoxton Hall), *Hidden* (Oval House) *Preserves* (Hen and Chickens Theatre); *Black Cab Music* (Lyric Hammersmith); True Stories (Central School of Speech of Drama). She held the position of Resident Assistant Director at The Gate, Notting Hill; credits for which include, *Joseph K, Fatherland* and *Electra*. Other credits as an Assistant Director: *The Revenger's Tragedy* (Hoxton Hall); *The Harder They Come: Concert* (TRSE); *Come Dancing: The Concert* (TRSE); *Crocodile* (Riverside Studios); *The Door Never Closes* (Almeida); *Britain's Got Bhangra* (UK Tour); *Bad Blood Blues, Come Dancing* (TRSE); *In His Hands*(Hackney Empire). She recently curated the exhibition *Re-introducing Oshun* for the Yinka Shonibare studio and is currently developing a new festival of digital work bridging the worlds of Art and Academia in Birmingham.

Ian Teague | *Designer*
Ian Teague trained in Theatre Design at what was then called Trent Polytechnic (now Nottingham Trent University) graduating in 1982. He has designed over 150 productions for a wide range of companies including Cardboard Citizens, MakeBelieve Arts, Eastern Angles, The London Bubble, Barking Broadway, Spare Tyre, Polka, Rose Bruford, Oxfordshire Touring, GYPT, Everyman Cheltenham, Action

Transport, Everyman Liverpool, 7:84, Dukes Theatre Lancaster, Torch Theatre Milford Haven, Durham Theatre Company, Forest Forge, Theatre Venture, Theatre Royal Stratford East and Nuffield Theatre Southampton. He is also a lecturer and workshop facilitator. His designs for small cast productions of Shakespeare formed part of the British Golden Triga winning entry at the Prague Quadrennial 2003. Ian has designed in a wide range of venues including theatres, schools, pubs, a football stadium, a park and Durham Cathedral but this is the first time he has designed a show on a farm.

Ciaran Cunningham | *Production Manager*
Ciarán trained at East 15 Acting School where he gained a BA Honors in Stage Management and Technical Theatre Theatre (Lighting Design). He then went on to work full time for Terry Tew Sound & Light Ltd and was also the Technical Manager at the Lion & Unicorn Theatre for 5 ½ years, which operates under Giant Olive Theatre. Now working as freelance Lighting Designer / Production Manager creating lighting Designs for Dance, Theatre & music, working with established artists and up & coming new companies and is Resident Lighting Technician at The Actors Church Covent Garden and The Tabernacle Notting Hill. He also has gone on to Lighting Design for Directors, Choreographers and Companies such as: Mark Baldwin, Richard Alston, Martin Lawrance, Jonathan Goddard, Antonia Franceschi, Patsy Rodenburg, Matthew Xia, Ella Mesma, Zoe Martlew, Simon Collier, Omar F Okai, Ray Shell, Shane Dempsey, New York Theatre Ballet, Ballet Black, Up and Over It, Chris Dugdale, Peter Oswald, NBA London, Urban Development, Fragments (International Ensemble), Church BoyZ, Black Gecko Dance Company and Community Arts North West.

Omar Okai | *Movement*
Omar is the Co-Founder and Artistic Director of the award-winning Okai Collier Company. His theatre directing / choreographic credits include: *Five Guys Named Moe* (Dir / Choreographer, The English Theatre Frankfurt); *Postcards from God: The Sister Wendy Musical* (Dir, Jermyn Street Theatre); *The Snow Queen* (Choreographer, Theatre Royal Stratford East); *Three Sisters* (Movement Direction, Birmingham Rep); *Preacherosity* (Dir, JST); *Sweet Charity* (Dir, Stratford Circus, re-staging Bob Fosse's original staging / choreography); *Rent* (Musical Staging, Frankfurt); *Purlie* (Dir, Bridewell, nominated for 4 What's On Stage Theatregoers Choice Awards 2005); *Cabaret* (Choreographer, Frankfurt); *Ruthless!* (Dir, Stratford Circus, winner of 5 Musical Stages awards 2002, including Best Director); *How To Succeed In Business Without Really Trying* (Dir, Rudolph Steiner); *High Heel Parrotfish!* (Choreographer, Theatre Royal Stratford East); *Honk*! (Dir, Rudolph Steiner); *Honk!* (Choreographer - National Tour); *Hoodies; A... My Name Is Alice; Elegies* (Bridewell / Three Mills); *Spooky Noises* (also book & lyrics); *Countess & Cabbages* (also book & lyrics); *A Time To Speak; Doing Something Right; Viva O Carnaval* (also book, song and lyrics); *Everyone's Opera; La Vie En Rose; Love Loss Life & Laughter; Child Of The Jago* (Purcell Room); *Carmen* (Movement Director, Lindbury Studio at The Royal Opera House); *Five Guys Named Moe* (Dir, William Ellis); *Burleigh Grimes* (Bridewell, Movement Director) & for the Royal National Theatre assistant Choreographer for the Olivier Award-winning *Honk!* and *The Villain's Opera.* Theatre producing credits include: *The Dorchester* (JST); *My Matisse* (JST); *The Crusaid Requiem* (St. Martin in the Fields) and *Passion* (Bridewell). Film directing

credits include: *The 411 – The Bottom Line On Amhurst Road.* West End performing credits: *Five Guys Named Moe* (Lyric, original cast), *Sweet Charity* (Victoria Palace), *King* and *My One And Only* (Piccadilly).

Connor Abbott | *Assistant Director*
Connor has trained with The National Youth Theatre and graduated from The University of York with a First Class Honours degree in Writing, Directing and Performance. Connor has directed numerous productions at university, including *The Provoked Wife* with Professor Michael Cordner and Dr Tom Cantrell. As assistant director, credits include *Blood and Chocolate* (Slung Low/Pilot Theatre/ York Theatre Royal). Connor has also developed theatre projects in schools and assisted in workshops with The National Youth Theatre. Connor is the artistic director of Outbreak Theatre and is currently in the process of preparing to direct an adaptation of La Ronde by Arthur Schnitzler. As a performer, Connor's credits include *Dorian* (Hinge Theatre, Edinburgh Fringe) and *Slick* (NYT).

Katie Thackery | *Stage Manager*
Katie trained at the Guildhall School of Music and Drama in Stage and Costume Management. Recent Stage Management credits include: Deputy Stage Manager on *Norma* at Opera Holland Park, Senior Stage Manager on *Secret Cinema 21: Miller's Crossing*, Assistant Stage Manager on *The Musketeers* for BBC Worldwide, Company Stage Manager on *Putting it Together* at the St James Theatre. In addition Katie has worked in costume on several films including *Edge of Tomorrow* for Warner Bros Pictures, and *Far From the Madding Crowd* for Fox Searchlight Pictures.

Nicola Alexis | *Daddy Love*
Since graduating from Mountview Theatre School, Nicola has appeared in numerous stage and screen productions. Notable Credits include *Lady in the Van,* (Salisbury Playhouse) Lead role in the Francis Matthews production *Lucky You*; Beauty in *Beauty and the Beast,* Masha in *Three Sisters* (Birmingham Rep); Clara Popkiss in *Rockery Nook* (dir. Dominic Dromgoole). Lead roles in original musicals, *G.I. Blues* & *One Love* (Bristol Old Vic). Nicola also performed in *Bacchai* directed by Sir Peter Hall (Royal National Theatre). Shakespeare roles include Bianca (*The Taming of the Shrew),* both Hermia and Tatiana *(A Midsummer Night's Dream)* and Portia *(The Merchant of Venice)*. Understudy roles *Jitney* (2002 Oliver Best New Play) and *Clybourne Park* (2012 Olivier Best New Play). Screen credits include; *Eastenders, Doctors, Holby City, Hollyoaks* and series regular in *The Bill* and feature role in BBC Film *Summerhill.*

Andreas Angelis | *Smoothy*
Andreas recently graduated from the musical theatre course at London College of Music. He was recently involved in a production of Joan Littlewood's *Oh What A Lovely War* where he was a part of the band as the drummer and various parts within the show as an actor. Andreas has been involved in several other musicals during his training, including a devised piece by Alex Loveless, *Bel Ami*, which run in the Charing Cross Theatre. As his inspiration, Andreas' dream is to emulate Al Pacino's career, from TV work to theatre. Andreas is very excited and honoured to be working with such a fantastic creative team and great cast, in his first professional credit since graduating.

Samuel Caseley | *Hero*
Samuel Caseley trained at the Central School of Speech and Drama and the University of Sussex. He has appeared in Serena Haywood's Pause with Moustache Contraption, Terrence McNally's *Corpus Christi* with Oufox Productions, has performed with The Writers' Guild Playwrights' Progress Project at the Leicester Square Theatre and has recently played in *Is It Getting Cold in Here?* at Theatre 503. He devised and wrote the play *Her Right Mind* with his company Rugged Isaac, which played at The Tabard Theatre and at the Brighton and Edinburgh Fringe Festivals. He has also appeared in several Short Films including Lloyd Eyre Morgan's *Broken Wings.*

Kevin Kinson | *Warrior*
Kevin Kinson started his acting career 16 years ago with Everyman Theatre and then quickly moved to work with the BBC with TV shows *Pobol Y Cwm*, *Satellite City*, *Yachi Da* and *Nuts & Bolts* before venturing into his first feature film with *Human Traffic*. Kevin trained at drama school in Manchester before forming his own theatre company and touring his own devised work throughout Europe including Serbia, Romania, Bilbao and Montenegro. Kevin has been in sell out shows in Edinburgh, Manchester and London, his most recent critically acclaimed performance, in Quentin Tarantino's *Reservoir Dogs*, completing its sell out run at the end of last year. Kevin's latest project, before *Revolution Farm*, was the feature film *Bang To Rights*, which is due for release in 2015. In addition to Kevin's acting work he is also an Award Winning Producer who has Produced and Executively Produced 7 feature films and a Double Award winning TV series.

Katie Arnstein | *Lil' Monster*

Katie is an actor and musician from the Midlands. Since graduating from Birmingham School of Acting in 2012 her stage roles have included Viola Meynall in Hound at The Riverside Studios, Fairy Bowbells in *Dick Whittington*, Madge in *Time and the Conways*, Peggy in *The London Cuckolds*, Presto in *Hey, Presto!* and most recently Lilly Jackson in *The Blonde Bombshells of 1943*. She has appeared in music videos for Kids in Glass Houses and The Watermelons and been the voice of Phoebe in *Letz Go Green*. She has taken part in The Mayor of London's "Gigs Big Busk" Scheme for two years playing the ukulele in a number of venues across London and was shortlisted for Best Original song. Katie is delighted to be involved with such a wonderful team of professionals and young people on Revolution Farm.

Newham City Farm

Opened in 1977, **Newham City Farm** is one of London's longest established and largest city farms. We are home to an extensive range of farmyard favourites and rare breeds – we have everything from a huge Shire Horse to tiny birds as well as cows, sheep, alpacas, goats, chickens, rabbits, fish, ferrets and even a Harris hawk. Find out more about the animals.

It's free for the general public to visit the farm and we are open every day except Monday all year round – we run special events throughout the year so make sure you check our events calendar to see what's on.

They might be the star attraction but there is much more to see at the farm than just the animals: there is an orchard, children's play area and picnic benches, as well as a café and a playbarn which will be opening very soon. We sell our produce too – you can often buy freshly laid eggs, honey from our bees, and even manure!

Schools and other groups are always welcome at a small charge, and we've got loads of ways to support your visit. We also have a range options for birthday parties and other celebrations.

Community Links

Community Links is an east London social action charity working with 16,000 people each year. It has over 35 years experience working in one of the most deprived, diverse and vibrant areas in the county. Today Community Links runs 40 social action projects, five social enterprises and three national campaigns. In 2013, projects provided challenging and inspirational activities for almost 8,000 children and young people; advised almost 5,000 people with benefits, housing and debt problems at a time when funding for this work is shrinking; supported around 4,000 unemployed people over a third of whom found suitable jobs, many more have gone onto further trained and voluntary work; worked with 177 young people excluded from mainstream education in its own Ofsted registered school, Education Links, increasing the GCSE pass rate by 7% and supported over 200 vulnerable ten and eleven year olds to make a successful transition to secondary school through its Opening Doors project. Community Links work is done with a staff team of permanent and sessional staff, many of whom are former service users, and volunteers from the local community and beyond.

CHARACTERS

OLD BOY

DADDY LOVE (BLACK PIG)

HERO (WHITE PIG)

SMOOTHY (PIG)

WARRIOR (STALLION)

LIL' MONSTER (MARE)

PIGEONHEAD

GOATFACE

BLACK SHEEP

DONKEYKICK

DUCKLIFE

RED HEN

COCKS X 2

SCENE ONE

Manor Farm. Midnight. Silence. Sound of an owl's call. And then movement. Slow at first, but gathering momentum. Indistinct shapes emerge from the dark and crawl, slither and creep towards the barn. These are the farm animals and a secret meeting has been called at midnight in the barn.

Old Boy *holds court in the middle of a semi-circle of animals. A sheep and goat keep lookout. They are checking on Mr Jones the farmer who's fallen into a drunken stupor. An air of nervous curiosity pervades the gathering.*

GOAT:	We good?
SHEEP:	We good. He's drunk.
GOAT:	What, again?
SHEEP:	Yeah. Wasteman.

They run to join the other animals.

GOAT:	It's all good.
SHEEP:	He's drunk.
YOUNG ANIMALS:	WHAT AGAIN???
PIG:	Back you go.
GOAT / SHEEP:	Dat ain't right!
STALLION:	Let 'em be.

The animals wait with bated breath. **Old Boy** *lifts his head towards the evening sky, takes a deep breath, and begins to address the assembled throng.*

OLD BOY: You know what…?

Pause

        I ain't got much to say…

Pause.

        …'cos at the end of it all, it's all a bloody big con ain' it…?

Pause.

        …yeah, a great big sloppy turd of a con.

Shock from the animals.

STALLION: Summin' on yer mind, Old Boy?

OLD BOY: Summin' like that.

STALLION: Spit it out then.

OLD BOY: I'm dyin', yous all know that.

MARE: Shut up. Don't talk like that.

OLD BOY: I ain't got no time for sentiment, sweetheart. Yous lot gotta get a move on. Gotta do summin'. I'm telling ya. If yous don't wanna end up like me. Worn out an' ready for the knife. Yeah, I'm old, I'm dying, I'm useless, no good to no one, so what? Way it's always been for the likes of us. *(pause)* But thing is, I keep havin' dreams, they won't go away, they haunt me, an' everyone of these dreams says: you was free once, Old Boy, you was free. And I have a picture of you, my friend, and you too sweetheart, running round them big fields, gentle breeze in your happy faces, blue sky above ya, pretty as a picture, no hunger, no starving, no beatings, yeah that's right… no humans…

…look around you, my friends…

…go on, have a good look…

…tell me, what 'd you see…?

…I'll tell you what I see. I see our land.

Pause

This is our land.

Pause.

Belongs to us.

Pause.

So why don't we take it?

An audible gasp among the younger animals.

STALLION: What sort of talk is that?

MARE: Daft talk if you ask me.

STALLION:	It ain't our land, Old Boy.
MARE:	Yeah, don't belong to us.
OLD BOY:	Don't it? I've said Yes Sir, No Sir all me life. Did what I was told to. Never questioned nuffin'. Always kept my head down. I was never any trouble. And what I've got to show for it? The knife, that's all. The knife. I want more. I want more to my life. I want it to mean summin' more than eating, shittin' an' sleepin' an' getting' ready to die. And why not? We do all the hard graft round here, but who grabs it, sells it, and makes a mint? The scum, that's who. But I reckon if we wanted to we could have it all. The fields, the grass, freedom, liberty – all ours. Yeah, I reckon we could have it all if we got rid of the scum…

Pause.

…yeah, that's right, take it over. Take over the farm.

Another gasp from the younger animals. Some of the older animals start whispering intently.

WHITE PIG:	Old Boy's right. We ain't been fed for weeks. Jones don't clean us out never. He hits the younguns. And I've slept in the same shit for three days!

PIG: Dangerous talk, my friend. You're talkin' about a riot. Smashin' the place up. Kickin' a few heads in. Could have serious repercussions that.

OLD BOY: *(pointing at groups of animals)* How long you got? A couple of years? Five years? Bit more? And you lot, how long you got? And you up there? Won't be long will it? Won't be long till your time's up. And it ain't your choice is it? Nah, it's theirs. They decide your fate.

He makes a slicing motion with his finger across his neck.

MARE: Shut up, Old Boy, you're frightening the younguns.

WHITE PIG: *(to* **Mare***)* That's how it is when you ain't free!

PIG: Alright, Old Boy, you made your point. We ain't in control. Never have been. We all know that. So what are you saying?

OLD BOY: I'm sayin' we fight back.

PIG: What with? Polite requests to kindly leave the farm?

The animals snigger.

OLD BOY: Ain't you ever noticed summin'?

PIG: What?

OLD BOY:	I mean, it's all around us, it's so simple.
PIG:	Yeah?
OLD BOY:	Yeah. We outnumber 'em.
PIG:	So?
OLD BOY:	So we chuck 'em out. Simple as that.

A sharp intake of breath among the animals.

> I mean, we're twice as strong as 'em. Right, Stallion?

STALLION:	Right, Old Boy!

*The animals start to realize the significance of what **Old Boy** has said.*

WHITE PIG:	Old Boy's right. An' it ain't jus' us. Neighbouring farms too. They'd join in. We'd proper slaughter the scum.
STALLION:	I could take 'em on me own!
WHITE PIG:	You could split 'em in half.
STALLION:	I could kick their heads in!
WHITE PIG:	You could break their backs.
STALLION:	I could smash their skulls to smithereens!
OLD BOY:	That's the spirit!
YOUNG ANIMALS:	*(chanting)* WARRIOR SMASH 'EM UP!

WARRIOR SMASH 'EM UP!

WARRIOR SMASH 'EM UP!

Black Pig *motions for quiet.*

PIG: Someone's needs to be in charge.

*They all turn to the **Black Pig**.*

WHITE PIG: What?

BLACK PIG: I said, someone needs to be in charge.

WHITE PIG: Of what exactly?

BLACK PIG: Of the revolution.

WHITE PIG: Ain't no one in charge of revolutions. That's the point.

BLACK PIG: Then you'll fail.

A shudder runs through the barn at this.

OLD BOY: Listen to me. We could work for ourselves. Working together. The lot of us. And mebbe, just mebbe, have some sort of life you could look back an' say yeah, it was well spent, it was my life, nobody else's, mine. all mine.

Old Boy *stares at the animals, eyes blazing.*

Man's the enemy. Always was. Always will be. Whose side are you on?

A knowing grin starts to spread across each of the animals' faces. And then a low, eerie chant goes up.

ALL: MAN'S THE ENEMY! KILL THE SCUM! CUT OFF HIS HEAD!

***White Pig** motions for quiet.*

WHITE PIG: He's got a gun.

OLD BOY: Yeah, and we got the darkness. A hundred pair of eyes in the night. Moving forward. In pitch black. He won't see a thing. Till it's too late.

Chant starts up again, low, eerie, sinister.

ALL: MAN'S THE ENEMY! KILL THE SCUM! CUT OFF HIS HEAD!

The animals start to crawl towards where Mr Jones is sleeping. It is a chilling, menacing sight. They chant under their breath as they creep and slide closer towards Mr Jones.

ALL: MAN'S THE ENEMY! KILL THE SCUM! CUT OFF HIS HEAD!

A huge commotion in the distance. The animals terrorise the farmer and his hired hands off the farm.

SCENE TWO

*They return to the barn victorious. Wild cheering and shouting. Primitive, tribal, frightening. A makeshift tomb of **Old Boy** lies in the middle of the barn.*

YOUNG ANIMALS: SMASH 'EM UP! BREAK THEIR BONES! KICK THEIR HEADS IN! SMASH 'EM UP! BREAK THEIR BONES! KICK THEIR HEADS IN! SMASH 'EM UP! BREAK THEIR BONES! KICK THEIR HEADS IN!

*They gather round **Stallion** eagerly.*

STALLION: You fought like tigers, soldiers. Proud of ya. Everyone of ya!!!

YOUNG ANIMALS: KILL THE SCUM! KILL THE SCUM! KILL THE SCUM!

WHITE PIG: That was for Old Boy. In memory of an old warrior. He freed us. Old Boy the warrior freed us!

YOUNG ANIMALS: OLD BOY THE WARRIOR! OLD BOY THE WARRIOR! OLD BOY THE WARRIOR!

WHITE PIG: See here, where Old Boy lies and rests. Honour this hero, this martyr, this starter of revolutions. He lived for battle, and died in battle. A minute's silence, brothers and sisters, for an old warrior.

They observe a minute's silence. The celebrations start up again.

***White Pig** winces.*

STALLION: You alright?

WHITE PIG: Ah, just a scratch.

STALLION: Get one of the soldiers to have a look at it.

WHITE PIG: It's nothing.

STALLION: All the same.

WHITE PIG: Easier than we thought eh?

STALLION: Element of surprise.

WHITE PIG: They'll be back.

STALLION: An' we'll be waitin' for em'. Right, soldiers?

YOUNG ANIMALS: SMASH 'EM UP! BREAK THEIR BONES! KICK THEIR HEADS IN! SMASH 'EM UP! BREAK THEIR BONES! KICK THEIR HEADS IN!

SMASH 'EM UP! BREAK THEIR BONES! KICK THEIR HEADS IN!

*Some of the younger animals are vandalizing the farm. The **Mare** confronts them.*

MARE: Hey! What you doin'?

ANIMALS: Whass it look like we doin'?

	Smashin' da place up!
MARE:	Why you doin' that?
ANIMALS:	'Cos it's da enemy!
	Yeah, scum innit!
MARE:	Fools!
ANIMALS:	You wha-?
MARE:	I said fools. Your destroyin' your own home. It's our farm now. We live here. Treat it with respect. Treat yourselves with respect. Go on, get lost. Now!

They skulk away, scowling and muttering under their breath.

Mare Joins Stallion.

MARE:	Did you have to charge in all by yourself?
STALLION:	Didn't see you holdin' back neither.
MARE:	It was a right laugh eh? The look on their faces.
STALLION:	Scarpered didn't they? Scarpered like frightened rabbits.
MARE:	And then we had the fields to ourselves.
STALLION:	All ours. All of 'em.
MARE:	Oh and we danced didn't we.
STALLION:	How we danced in the fields.

MARE: We ran about everywhere, like we'd just learnt how to gallop, like we was young and foolish and silly again, and had all the time in the world.

STALLION: And no one could touch us, and like Old Boy said, we was doing what we wanna do, what we was born to do.

MARE: We was free for the first time in our lives, and it felt good.

White Pig has grabbed a loudhailer, and is whipping up the animals into a frenzy.

WHITE PIG: Brothers and sisters, the time had come when each and everyone of us had to decide whether we are gonna be the problem or whether we are gonna be the solution. And we decided we were gonna be the solution! We chose, brothers and sisters! We chose!

Wild cheering, whooping, noises.

I want everybody to get up and make some noise. I wanna hear some revolution out there! Make some noise! Make some noise! Brothers and sisters I wanna hear the revolution out there. I wanna hear some noise. Are you ready! Are you ready!

The animals go berserk.

White Pig snarls and broods.

STALLION: Whassa matter? Ain't joinin' in?

WHITE PIG: I still got a scum name. You still got one. We all still got scum names.

STALLION: Joey? Don't mean nuthin' to me.

MARE: April Babe? Wot is that??? Yuk!!!

WHITE PIG: Freckles. That's the worse.

MARE: So let's change 'em. Let's get rid of 'em!

STALLION: Nice, I like it.

WHITE PIG: Only one name for you – Warrior.

STALLION: Happy wiv that.

MARE: I wanna be Lil' Monster.

WHITE PIG: What?

MARE: Don't get on the wrong side of me.

STALLION: True, very true.

MARE: And you?

STALLION: Hero. That's what you woz in the battle.

WHITE PIG: *(seeing two pigs)* What about them two?

STALLION: Smoothy. Talks smooth. Talks fancy.

PIG: I hate to break up the party...

STALLION: Hold up, we was just choosin' new names for ourselves, you know, now we run

	things an' all. I'm Warrior, she's Lil' Monster, he's Hero, and we thought we'd call you Smoothy.
PIG:	Smoothy?
STALLION:	On account of you being a smooth talker.
PIG:	I'm flattered
WHITE PIG:	What about you?

Black Pig thinks about it.

BLACK PIG:	Daddy Love. 'Cos I got so much love in here for you. You're my family.

They make fierce noises/movements representing solidarity and togetherness.

SMOOTHY:	We've been thinking, we need rules.
HERO:	O yeah?
SMOOTHY:	Now the farm is ours. We need rules.
HERO:	Dunno if I like the sound of that.
SMOOTHY:	Can't live without rules. Not possible. Not unless you want anarchy.
HERO:	You what?
SMOOTHY:	Anarchy. No one in charge. Everybody fending for themselves. Stabbing. Gouging. Biting. Just for a stupid apple or

a carrot. That's what you get if you don't have rules.

DONKEYKICK: You hear that? We definitely need rules!

GOATFACE: Yeah, no one's bitin' me that's for sure.

HERO: What kind of rules you talkin' about?

DADDY LOVE: Rules we must all obey.

HERO: That was the old way.

SMOOTHY: The old way? Don't talk to me about the old ways. The revolting, disgusting, filthy old ways! They're gone for ever. Right, soldiers?

ALL: GONE FOR EVER! GONE FOR EVER! GONE FOR EVER!

SMOOTHY: What isn't gone for ever though is the scum. They could come back any time, in fact they could be planning a vicious attack right this minute... we need rules to help us... be safe... be ready... be prepared...

The animals peer around the farm nervously.

...be afraid, brothers and sisters, be very afraid... the scum are watching you...

The animals nod in unison.

	...no getting away from it, rules are good, rules are useful, rules –
DADDY LOVE:	– must be obeyed.
HERO:	So you're in charge now, eh?
DADDY LOVE:	We're all in charge.
HERO:	But you two are doing most of the talkin'.
DADDY LOVE:	Feel free to join in, my friend.
HERO:	Rules are what scum do.
DADDY LOVE:	Scum ain't in charge now. We are.
HERO:	And we can do what we like.
SMOOTHY:	What Daddy Love is saying is rules help us organise.
	Manage effectively.
	Administer efficiently.
	Facilitate smoothly.
	Streamline purposefully.

*The animals stare blank-faced at **Daddy Love** and **Smoothy**, bewildered by these words.*

	O didn't we tell you? We've taught ourselves to read and write.
LIL' MONSTER:	When d'you do that?

SMOOTHY: Couple of months ago. The scum's gotta good library.

LIL' MONSTER: *(sarcastically)* That's nice.

SMOOTHY: Well, aren't you pleased? We did it for you. For us. For the revolution. So we can beat the scum at their own game.

WARRIOR: Well, go on then, yous the brainy ones. What are these rules? See if we like 'em.

DADDY LOVE: All animals are the same.

WARRIOR: All animals are the same?

SMOOTHY: Yes. All the same.

WARRIOR: Don't have a problem wiv that.

GOATFACE: What, even rats?

SMOOTHY: Even rats.

DONKEYKICK: Dunno about that.

DADDY LOVE: *(sternly)* Even rats.

SMOOTHY: Surely Hero cannot be unhappy with the principle of equality? Or Daddy Lovism, if you like.

HERO: Daddy Lovism?

SMOOTHY: Well, it was Daddy's idea, and it is rather a good one, don't you think?

HERO: What about Old Boyism?

SMOOTHY: Old Boyism?

HERO: It was Old Boy who inspired the revolution. It was his idea. Why don't we call it Old Boyism?

SMOOTHY: Old Boy is dead.

HERO: All the more reason we should honour his legacy.

SMOOTHY: Daddy Lovism is about everybody being equal. I think you'll find Old Boyism was about working for ourselves.

HERO: So?

SMOOTHY: So there's a subtle difference. We think Daddy Lovism is the more important part.

WARRIOR: Who cares who said it. You just tell us what to do. You're the brains.

SMOOTHY: We good?

Hero frowns. He wants to assert his part in the revolution.

HERO: Old Boyism calls for re-education of the masses! All animals must learn basic skills in writing and reading.

DUCKLIFE: *(groaning)* Oh no, he's jokin' right?

RED HEN: I thought we was supposed to be free?

The animals slope off whinging to each other.

SCENE THREE

Classroom. The animals are having reading and writing classes. Hullabaloo, commotion; **Hero's** *barely able to control the class.*

HERO: Class, settle down please.

The class eventually settles.

Brothers and sisters, remember this, we are nothing without knowledge.

Knowledge will set you free. Knowledge will build you up. Knowledge will make you bigger and better than before. But remember this too, brothers and sisters, knowledge is power, and power must be used responsibly.

Yawns from the animals.

Warrior, would you read please?

WARRIOR: Why me?

HERO: Because I'm asking you.

WARRIOR: You'll be lucky.

Warrior *struggles with the words on the page, he can't make head or tail of it, exasperated he tosses the book to the floor.*

Nah, it's no good, I can't do it!

LIL' MONSTER: Warrior!

Warrior *storms off.*

DUCKLIFE:	Can I go as well, Sir?
RED HEN:	An' me, Sir?
HERO:	No. Right, spelling. The 'i' before 'e' rule. 'i' before 'e' except after 'c', but only when it rhymes with 'bee'. Example 1. 'Believe' The 'i' sound rhymes with bee, so 'I' goes before 'e'.
DUCKLIFE:	Who cares!
HERO:	It's important.
RED HEN:	How we supposed to remember all that, Sir?
HERO:	'i' before 'e' except after 'c', but only when it rhymes with 'bee'.
BLACK SHEEP:	But Sir, what if I never use them words? Does that I mean I don't have to learn 'em?
HERO:	Don't you want to learn to spell?
BLACK SHEEP:	What for?
HERO:	So you can educate yourself.
BLACK SHEEP:	But we're free ain't we?
HERO:	Don't you want a better future for yourself?
BLACK SHEEP:	Daddy and Smoothy'll look after us. They said so.

HERO: And what if they can't?

BLACK SHEEP: What are you saying, Sir? That Daddy and Smoothy ain't heroes of the revolution? That they ain't gonna take care of us? That ain't very loyal of you.

HERO: No, I'm not saying that.

BLACK SHEEP: That's what you said.

HERO: No, I said education is a good thing because you can better yourself, improve yourself, you don't have to rely on others to help you.

BLACK SHEEP: Have you told 'em that, Sir?

HERO: What?

BLACK SHEEP: That you don't wanna rely on others, that you'd rather do your own thing? Are you a rebel, Sir? Is that what you are?

HERO: Don't distort my words. Spelling, let's continue. Prefixes and suffixes. Prefixes and suffixes are used to make new words.

PIGEONHEAD: This is boring.

RED HEN: Yeah, forget it.

LIL' MONSTER: *(rounding on the class)* Hey, shut up willya, I'm tryin' to learn summin' here!

*The class immediately quietens down. But one of the animals throws something at **Lil' Monster**. She gets up and hits the culprit. All hell breaks loose.*

PIGEONHEAD: I'm outta here!

RED HEN: Same here!

The animals start to leave.

HERO: Class! Sit down! Where are you going?

Smoothy saunters in.

The class return to their seats immediately.

SMOOTHY: Good Morning, Hero. And how is our re-education programme going? How is class today?

ALL: BORING!!!

SMOOTHY: O dear.

HERO: They're a little resistant. This is what the scum have done to them. Kept them in the dark. Kept them down. Kept them ignorant. Brother, I will awaken their minds, I will bring them into the light. I will make them see the truth.

SMOOTHY: Carry on, brother.

Smoothy sits down at the back of the classroom and starts making notes.

Ignore me. I'm not here.

HERO: Prefixes and suffixes. You add prefixes and suffixes to a word to change its meaning. A prefix goes where?

DUCKLIFE: Do what???

RED HEN: What's he say?

All hells breaks loose again.

SMOOTHY: *(to Hero)* May I?

He motions for quiet.

Class, repeat after me: Four legs badass, two legs wasteman.

ALL: FOUR LEGS BADASS, TWO LEGS WASTEMAN!

SMOOTHY: Very good. What does it mean?

GOATFACE: Easy. Man is scum!

SMOOTHY: Well done. And what does Revolution Farm mean to you?

DONKEYKICK: It means a punch up!

SMOOTHY: Good work class, good work.

HERO: It's slang.

SMOOTHY: It's what they understand.

HERO: But that's not education.

SMOOTHY: Easy to remember though isn't it?

HERO: And what about reading and writing?

SMOOTHY: Is it strictly necessary? I mean, they're not exactly leadership material are they?

HERO: Ain't the point.

SMOOTHY: Hero, we need the muscle, remember. 'Case the scum come back. Books will only confuse 'em. And we need them focussed. Ready to attack at a moment's notice.

HERO: They're not an army, Smoothy.

SMOOTHY: Army's the most important thing in the revolution. Get them on your side and you're away. *(to class)* Soldiers of the revolution, I salute you! Are you ready for battle? Are you ready for war? Are you ready for bloodshed?

ALL: YES WE ARE! YES WE ARE! YES WE ARE!

SMOOTHY: Class. These are the new rules. Learn them by heart. Recite them day and night.

This is how we live. This is Revolution Farm.

Man is scum!

ANIMALS: MAN IS SCUM!

SMOOTHY: Animals are not scum!

ANIMALS: ANIMALS ARE NOT SCUM!

SMOOTHY: Clothes are what scum wear!

ANIMALS: CLOTHES ARE WHAT SCUM WEAR!

SMOOTHY: Beds are what scum sleep in!

ANIMALS: BEDS ARE WHAT SCUM SLEEP IN!

SMOOTHY: Alcohol is what scum drink!

ANIMALS: ALCOHOL IS WHAT SCUM DRINK!

SMOOTHY: Killing each other is what scum do!

ANIMALS: KILLING EACH OTHER IS WHAT SCUM DO!

SMOOTHY: All animals are the same!

ANIMALS: ALL ANIMALS ARE THE SAME!

SMOOTHY: Thank you, class. Carry on, Hero. *(whispering)* Go easy on the grammar, eh? *(He winks at **Hero**.)*

*He turns to go. **Lil' Monster** stands in his way.*

LIL' MONSTER: Ain't see you for a while.

SMOOTHY: Busy, busy, busy.

LIL' MONSTER: Doin' what?

SMOOTHY: This an' that.

LIL' MONSTER: Where's Daddy Love?

SMOOTHY: Around.

LIL' MONSTER: Nice if he could pop in once or twice.

SMOOTHY: Anything the matter?

LIL' MONSTER: What you doin' wiv them puppies?

SMOOTHY: Ah, who can resist 'em? Adorable little things.

LIL' MONSTER: Gonna give em back then?

SMOOTHY: First things first.

*He leans into **Lil' Monster**.*

Let me let you into a little secret.

Whispers into her ear.

Education. Get 'em while their young eh?

He winks at her.

A goat and donkey come tearing in.

GOATFACE: They're comin'! They're comin'!

DONKEYKICK: They got pitchforks, sticks, clubs!

SMOOTHY: Warrior! Where's Warrior? Somebody call Warrior!

YOUNG ANIMALS: KILL THE SCUM! KILL THE SCUM! KILL THE SCUM!

Warrior *tears in.*

SMOOTHY: The scum is back, Warrior. Marshall your troops and wait for our orders. I'll get Daddy Love.

He dashes off.

WARRIOR: Who fought in the revolution?

DONKEYKICK: We did.

WARRIOR: You'll be with me. Stay by my side.

GOATFACE: They got weapons.

WARRIOR: If we stick together, we'll be alright. They wanna break us up. Pick us off one by one. Don't let 'em do that. Hold the line. You hear me. Hold the line. We work together.

ALL: TOGETHER!

TOGETHER!

TOGETHER!

SCENE FOUR

The animals charge off to fight the men. Several hours later the animals return, bloody and brusied, but victorious. Mr Jones and his men have been defeated. **Warrior** *dresses* **Lil' Monster's** *wounds.*

LIL' MONSTER: I'm alright!

WARRIOR: You're bleeding badly

LIL' MONSTER: It's nothin'.

WARRIOR: Stand still!

LIL' MONSTER: We all made it?

HERO: We lost a few.

WARRIOR: I told 'em to hold the line.

HERO: Smaller ones. No chance. Scum had weapons.

WARRIOR: You hurt?

HERO: A few cuts, that's all.

Pause.

Warrior...

WARRIOR: Yeah?

HERO: The farmboy...

WARRIOR: What about him?

HERO: He ain't movin'…

WARRIOR: Would've done the same to us. *(to the animals)* You did well, soldiers.

The younger animals beam with pride.

ALL: HOLD THE LINE! HOLD THE LINE! HOLD THE LINE!

PIGEONHEAD: They was mental.

RED HEN: Mad, I tell you.

PIGEONHEAD: Took five of 'em down.

RED HEN: All over 'em like a rash.

LIL' MONSTER: Who?

PIGEONHEAD: Daddy and Smoothy 'course.

LIL' MONSTER: Did you see 'em?

PIGEONHEAD: That's what dem pigeons an' hens said.

RED HEN: Said they fought like monsters innit.

PIGEONHEAD: Had to be dragged away.

LIL' MONSTER: *(to Warrior)* You see 'em?

WARRIOR: I confess I was a little busy, my dear, and may have been distracted – pounding the scum's heads in!

A big cheer goes up at this. **Daddy Love** *and* **Smoothy** *stagger in, bleeding and bruised.*

Black Sheep rushes to help them

SMOOTHY: Please. It's alright, we're alright.

BLACK SHEEP: What happened?

SMOOTHY: We was ambushed.

WARRIOR: Ambushed? Where?

SMOOTHY: On the lane down to Hillside.

LIL' MONSTER: That's miles from the farm.

SMOOTHY: We had 'em on the run. But the scum was waitin' for us. Didn't' stand a chance. Daddy took the brunt of it.

BLACK SHEEP: Let's get 'em! Bust 'em up!

WARRIOR: You ain't goin' nowhere! (t*o Daddy Love and Smoothy*).

You get better get some rest.

DADDY LOVE: No. Just a few broken ribs that's all. Tonight we celebrate. Celebrate our victory. I just want to be with you. My soldiers. My family.

He groans in pain. It's all fake, but the animals are taken in.
***Black Sheep** darts towards **Daddy** and **Smoothy**.*

BLACK SHEEP: Brothers, please let me dress your wounds. I would be honoured.

Wild cheering, victory celebrations etc.

SCENE FIVE

The barn. The animals are lazily chatting away.

DONKEYKICK: Hero's says he's gonna build a windmill.

GOATFACE: A what?

DONKEYKICK: A windmill.

GOATFACE: What's a windmill?

DONKEYKICK: It's wicked. Gonna do all the work for us. I swear down we be doin' a three-day week soon.

GOATFACE: Serious?

DONKEYKICK: Serious.

GOATFACE: I like that.

DONKEYKICK: Electrics ain' it. Electrics means we don't have to do the work.

GOATFACE: How's that?

DONKEYKICK: I dunno. Do I look like a windmill expert? Anyways, Hero's goin' round sayin' dis means we won't have to work so hard, mebbe only three days a week, mebbe even less, electrics do it all for us. He's locked himself away, don't talk to nobody, just draws an' draws, like he's gone mad or summin'.

GOATFACE:	He's the boss, no doubt. He won us the Battle of Revolution Farm.
PIGEONHEAD:	Fool! Warrior won it, he smashed it, Warrior always smashes it, you know that.
BLACK SHEEP:	Daddy Love and Smoothy, it was dem. They was ready to die, tellin' ya!
DUCKLIFE:	I dunno, I'm confused, we got a lot of leaders we have.
RED HEN:	Don't think. You're not good at that.

They continue to bicker, argue.

LIL' MONSTER:	Listen to 'em. Don't know what they talkin' about.
WARRIOR:	Leave 'em be.
LIL' MONSTER:	You know they knick the milk?
WARRIOR:	You what?
LIL' MONSTER:	Daddy and Smoothy. They're nickin' the milk. An' the apples. I seen 'em.
WARRIOR:	Don't be daft.
LIL' MONSTER:	I seen 'em. They're keepin' it for themselves.
WARRIOR:	Rubbish.
LIL' MONSTER:	Suit yourself.

WARRIOR: Why would they do that? They're one of us. You know, all animals are the same an' all that. It don't make no sense.

LIL' MONSTER: We don't see 'em much these days.

WARRIOR: Busy ain't they.

LIL' MONSTER: Doin' what?

WARRIOR: I dunno. Sortin' the farm out. Reading all them books of theirs. Who cares?

LIL' MONSTER: Why's it gotta be them sorting things out?

WARRIOR: Well, I ain't gonna sort it out.

LIL' MONSTER: That's what I'm talkin' about. We never do nothin'. We just let others do it for us.

WARRIOR: Look, we free now ain't we? Harvest's come in. Got plenty to eat. Everyone's happy. Long as we work hard and work together we're aright. Who cares who does what?

LIL' MONSTER: Yeah, suppose so...

WARRIOR: You think about things too much, that's your trouble.

Black Sheep imitates Daddy Love

BLACK SHEEP: I'm Daddy Love! I'll kill ya! I'll kill ya! Kill the lot o' ya!

Goatface imitates Hero.

GOATFACE: I'm Hero! Who's wants some?! You want some?! What about you?!

A scuffle ensues.

WARRIOR: Hey, pack it in!

The animals growl at each other.

LIL' MONSTER: How's the reading going?

WARRIOR: Leave it out.

LIL' MONSTER: Well?

WARRIOR: Well what?

LIL' MONSTER: How's it going?

WARRIOR: It ain't.

LIL' MONSTER. Read to me.

WARRIOR: Nah.

LIL' MONSTER: O, Warrior, you're supposed to be studying!

WARRIOR: I tried alright.

LIL' MONSTER: What happened?

WARRIOR: Don't make no sense. Big words. Give me a headache.

LIL' MONSTER: You gotta practice.

WARRIOR: What good is it?

LIL' MONSTER: So you can know things.

WARRIOR: What things?

LIL' MONSTER: Things we don't know about.

WARRIOR: What d'you know then?

Lil' Monster's embarrassed.

LIL' MONSTER: Yeah, alright, big words, they're horrible ain't they. Gives me a headache too.

WARRIOR: Dunno if it's for us, Lil' Monster, don't feel right

LIL' MONSTER: At least I'm tryin'.

Lil' Monster sighs.

GOATFACE: Hey, Warrior, what d'you think? Hero's windmill?

WARRIOR: Work hard, you lot, that's the main thing. Work till you drop.

ALL: WORK TILL WE DROP! WORK TILL WE DROP! WORK TILL WE DROP!

Daddy Love and Smoothy enter. they are dressed in formal attire. they set up a table and chairs for themselves on a raised platform.

SMOOTHY: Order! Order! I call this meeting to order. Silence please! Thank you. We have called this meeting today to discuss a very important matter. A matter that affects each and everyone of us and therefore it is only right we all have a say in it. I shall act as your Chair and as such it is my responsibility for ensuring the smooth running of the meeting. The question of whether or not to begin work on the windmill. We will put it to the vote.

GOATFACE: 'Scuse me.

SMOOTHY: What is it? The meeting's started.

GOATFACE: Why you wearing clothes?

DONKEYKICK: Yeah, 'gainst the rules ain't it?

ALL: CLOTHES ARE WHAT SCUM WEAR!

SMOOTHY: Quite right. Clothes are what scum wear – except when such is the gravitas and importance of the occasion only a formal attire will suffice.

PIGEONHEAD: Eh?

RED HEN: What's he say?

SMOOTHY: Clothes are what scum wear – 'cept when there's urgent decisions to be made. Happy now? I call this meeting open. Hero, you may speak first.

Hero steps forward to address the meeting.

HERO: Thank you, Brother.

SMOOTHY: Please address me as Chair.

HERO: Thank you, Chair. Soldiers of the revolution, it is my great honour to present to you –

Hero whips off a sheet on a blackboard to unveil a drawing of the windmill.

Revolution Farm's first Electricity Generating Windmill!

General bewilderment from the animals.

Brothers and sisters, this is nothing less than a liberation, a liberation from the evil tyranny of non-stop work. Rejoice in the power of the windmill to release you from your drudgery, your enslavement, your imprisonment!

Cheering, whooping etc.

Smoothy motions for silence.

SMOOTHY: Daddy Love, would you care to respond?

Daddy Love steps forwards.

DADDY LOVE: Crap.

He sits down again.

SMOOTHY: It would appear Daddy Love has made his comments.

Hero seizes the moment and comes forward again.

HERO: With this windmill, all who live on Revolution Farm will finally be free. We will dance in the fields again, we will play again, we will laugh and sing and be happy and be free again!

A wild chant of 'Build the windmill' goes up among the animals.

Daddy Love *utters a high-pitched scream and a pack of ferocious dogs come tearing in and make for* ***Hero****, who leaps out of the barn and only just manages to escape. the animals are in a state of shock.* ***Warrior*** *immediately leaps up and confronts* ***Daddy Love***.

WARRIOR: That was out of order.

DADDY LOVE: You're in my face, Warrior.

WARRIOR: You was out of order.

DADDY LOVE: O, well, what's done is done.

Daddy's *attack dogs circle* ***Warrior****, slowly and methodically. A tense stand-off.* ***Lil' Monster*** *quickly intervenes.*

LIL' MONSTER: Warrior… leave it, c'mon.

She leads him away gently. None of the animals says a word. They are all too shocked. They comfort each other in groups.

SCENE SIX

The animals are discussing recent events on the farm. Some of them are noticeably thinner/weaker by now.

GOATFACE: So we gonna build it after all?

DONKEYKICK: That's what Smoothy says yeah.

GOATFACE: But I thought they said no?

RED HEN: Yeah, Daddy said crap.

DUCKLIFE: Nah, Smoothy says it was Daddy's idea all along – Hero knicked it off him.

GOATFACE: Serious?

DUCKLIFE: No joke.

BLACK SHEEP: I always thought there was summin' funny about him.

GOATFACE: Who?

BLACK SHEEP: You know who I'm talkin' 'bout.

GOATFACE: Hero?

BLACK SHEEP: Yeah.

GOATFACE: What you talkin' about, fool?

BLACK SHEEP: Don't call me fool. I'll tell Daddy you called me that.

GOATFACE: What kind of name is Daddy Love?

BLACK SHEEP: 'Cos he's like a Father to us. We're his children. He'll look after us. He'll protect us. Some of us anyway...

PIGEONHEAD: Thing is, right, Hero won us the Battle of the Cowshed, right?

DUCKLIFE: Yeah, but Smoothy says he found all these plans in the shed by Hero 'bout takin' over the farm. He shut himself away right? Didn't come out for days. What was he doin' den?

RED HEN: Smoothy says we gotta be on guard for anything, anyone... even traitors...

BLACK SHEEP: (*to Goatface*) I saw you, you laughed when I said Daddy was like a Father.

GOATFACE: So?

BLACK SHEEP: Be careful.

GOATFACE: Or what?

BLACK SHEEP: Jus' sayin'.

GOATFACE: Jus' sayin' what?

BLACK SHEEP: Jus' sayin' be careful.

They square up to each other.

LIL' MONSTER: Alright, pack it in you two!

Goatface *and* ***Black Sheep*** *separate.*

	(to **Warrior***)* You hear 'em? Well, what d'you think now?
WARRIOR:	What you mean?
LIL' MONSTER:	They sayin' Hero's a traitor.
WARRIOR:	Alright, Daddy was bang out of order, I didn't like it and I said so, but the thing is, if Hero was up to summin' –
LIL' MONSTER:	Warrior!
WARRIOR:	Look, the revolution comes first, that's what Smoothy's always sayin'.
LIL' MONSTER:	Hero was tryin' help us!
WARRIOR:	Them two know what they're doin'. They're the brains.
LIL' MONSTER:	No, they're the thought-workers.
WARRIOR:	You what?
LIL' MONSTER:	That's what they're callin' themselves these days. An' that's not all, they're sayin' thought workers need lots of rest and food so they can think better. What's that mean?
WARRIOR:	I dunno, let 'em get on with it.
LIL' MONSTER:	That's what you always say.
WARRIOR:	Well, what d' you want me to say? That Warrior's got the answer? Warrior knows

	what to do? Warrior's gotta plan? That ain't me. I ain't like that. Let 'em get on wiv it.
LIL' MONSTER:	And the dogs? What about the dogs?
WARRIOR:	It ain't right. But there's work to do.
LIL' MONSTER:	*(wearily)* Yeah, I know Warrior, gotta work harder, work till you drop – and then you die.
WARRIOR:	Don't talk daft. No one's gonna die. Warrior's tough. Warrior's strong. Warrior's bigger an' fitter than all the rest.
LIL' MONSTER:	He won't always be bigger an' fitter.
WARRIOR:	I won't let you down, Lil'. I promise.

She turns her head away.

You think I could live with that?

She's upset

You know me, you know me through an' through.

She softens.

Gissus a smile. Come on. I knows you can do it.

She smiles.

There ya go!

Warrior *struts and parades among the animals, flaunting his strength and power to the delight of the younger animals.*

WARRIOR: WHO'S THE HARDEST OF 'EM ALL?

ALL: WARRIOR! WARRIOR! WARRIOR!

SCENE SEVEN

The animals are working hard to build the windmill. ***Warrior****, as ever, is overdoing it.*

ALL:	WORK TILL YOU DROP! WORK TILL YOU DROP! WORK TILL YOU DROP!
LIL' MONSTER:	You're overdoin' it again.
WARRIOR:	It's gotta be built.
LIL' MONSTER:	But you never stop.
WARRIOR:	An' I won't stop till it's done.
ALL:	WORK TILL YOU DROP! WORK TILL YOU DROP! WORK TILL YOU DROP!
LIL' MONSTER:	O shut up willya! The lot of you!

An animal slips and injures themself.

> Warrior, it ain't safe.

WARRIOR: Alright, break!

The animals take a break.

LIL' MONSTER: We work harder than ever, but we eat less than ever. This ain't how it was supposed to be. Where's all the food gone? The Harvest?

There was plenty once.

WARRIOR: It don't last for ever.

LIL' MONSTER: No, not if you're pinchin' it for yourself.

WARRIOR: O leave off.

LIL' MONSTER: Look at the state of them, poor things.

WARRIOR: Hey, you two, take a break alright?

GOATFACE: No, we cool.

DONKEYKICK: Yeah, we good.

LIL' MONSTER: They're just tryin' to impress you.

WARRIOR: Well, what d'you want me to do?

LIL' MONSTER: I want you to take it easy.

WARRIOR: Warrior don't do easy.

LIL' MONSTER: No, Warrior. don't do nothin'.

WARRIOR: *(angrily)* Enough! Right!

*Warrior carries on working, harder than before. **Daddy Love** and **Smoothy** saunter in, and the atmosphere palpably changes. The animals tense up.*

SMOOTHY: Ah it looks splendid, brothers and sisters, it looks splendid. A little way to go of course, but magnificent, truly magnificent. Oh look at the smile on Daddy's face! He's so proud of you. Well, I know you're all raring to get back to work, so we won't keep you long. Daddy has an important announcement to make. One that will benefit each and everyone of us. One that will consolidate our glorious, heroic revolution and open up a brand new world to us. And guess whose bright idea it was? Well, I think you know the answer to that. Ahem. *(coughs, clears his throat)* We're going to trade with the humans.

GOATFACE: Ain't man the enemy?

DONKEYKICK: Always was. Always will be. That's what Old Boy said.

RED HEN: True dat.

DADDY LOVE: *(screaming)* Don't ever say that name again! You hear me! Never again! I forbid you to ever mention his name again! *(collecting himself together, he strokes their faces gently)* I find the mere mention of his name painful. He was a like a Father to me. But I am the Father now. Life goes on.

The animals visibly wilt.

LIL' MONSTER: Work with humans? Ain't it against the rules?

SMOOTHY: Which rule is that?

LIL' MONSTER: Man is scum

SMOOTHY: Man is scum yes, except when it's absolutely necessary. And right now don't you think it's absolutely necessary? Who wants to get fed?

All hands go up very quickly.

RED HEN: Smoothy's right. I'm starving.

PIGEONHEAD: Yeah, me too.

DUCKLIFE: Anyone seen a rat?

GOATFACE: Killing each other is what scum do!

RED HEN: 'Cept when it's absolutely necessary.

SMOOTHY: Brothers and sisters, the simple truth is we need human things, materials, tools, things we can't produce for ourselves, and we need 'em now. The sooner that windmill goes up, the sooner we can all reap the benefits of our glorious revolution.

WARRIOR: The younguns are done in – give 'em a day off.

SMOOTHY: Of course. But d'you really think that's wise? Well, I don't wish to alarm anyone, and it's only a rumour of course, but word is going round that the scum are joining forces and meeting up on a regular basis… I think they're up to something…

DUCKLIFE: *(frightened)* Are they comin' back then?

SMOOTHY: Are you afraid, brother?

DUCKLIFE: A bit.

SMOOTHY: They killed your friend didn't they?

DUCKLIFE: Yeah.

SMOOTHY: How does that make you feel?

DUCKLIFE: Bad. I got some bad thoughts.

SMOOTHY: What would your friend want you to do?

DUCKLIFE: Kill 'em!

*He embraces **Ducklife** and kisses him on the forehead.*

LIL' MONSTER: We could do with some help.

SMOOTHY: What use am I? I'm hopeless at these things, they require practical skills. I'd only be a hindrance, in your way, mucking things up. No, we need the experts. Right, Warrior?

WARRIOR: Well, I ain't no expert.

SMOOTHY: No expert, he says! Did you hear that? Oh you are funny, Warrior. No, Warrior, you *are* the farm. You're the heart and soul of it. We're depending on you. And you know what? When it's built, I think we'll call it Warrior's Windmill. In honour of all your magnificent work.

WARRIOR: Well thanks but... well everyone's doing their bit right, I mean we're all doing our bit.

SMOOTHY: No, I insist, we'll call it Warrior's Windmill.

YOUNG ANIMALS: WARRIOR'S WINDMILL!

WARRIOR'S WINDMILL!

WARRIOR'S WINDMILL!

Warrior is visibly proud.

WARRIOR: See Lil' Monster, I ain't stupid after all. I done summin'!

DADDY LOVE: My favourite son is an example to us all.

Daddy Love bestows a kiss on Warrior.

Warrior turns to the animals.

WARRIOR: Well, what you waitin' for? Work you till you drop!

Warrior and the animals continue to work furiously.

ALL: WORK TILL YOU DROP! WORK TILL YOU DROP! WORK TILL YOU DROP!

SCENE EIGHT

The animals are celebrating the completion of the windmill. It is pandemonium inside the barn, primitive, almost shamanistic.

ALL: WINDMILL'S UP! WINDMILL'S UP! WINDMILL'S UP!

Suddenly there is a huge crash. The windmill has collapsed in the storm. The animals freeze. **Donkeykick** *shoots out and returns almost immediately.*

DONKEYKICK: The windmill – it's gone!

WARRIOR: What???

DONKEYKICK: It's fallen down!

Daddy Love *emits a high pitched scream.*

DADDY LOVE: Hero!!!!

Daddy Love's *attack dogs come running in. All the animals freeze.*

SMOOTHY: It was Hero. Hero's sabotaged our glorious windmill.

WARRIOR: Don't make no sense. Why'd he do that?

SMOOTHY: You mean you don't know?

WARRIOR: Don't know what?

SMOOTHY: He was working with 'em, Warrior.

WARRIOR: With who?

SMOOTHY: The scum of course.

WARRIOR: Hero..?

LIL' MONSTER: Don't be stupid. Hero was one o' us.

SMOOTHY: Stupid am I ? Then how stupid is this?

Smoothy whips out several pieces of paper and throws them at Lil' Monster.

> We discovered these among his plans for the windmill. Would you care to read them out aloud for us, please?

LIL' MONSTER: *(struggling to read)* I... I... can't... Warrior... can you...?

Warrior shakes his head, embarrassed.

SMOOTHY: Oh, I beg your pardon, you two can't read can you? Well, let me help you out. *(reading)* "When I'm the Great Leader of Revolution Farm, I'll kill Daddy Love and Smoothy and anybody that gets in my way. Lil' Monster trusts me completely and Warrior, well, Warrior's just an idiot. So no worries there. And I've got the humans on my side. Mr Jones is just waiting for me to give the word. What a surprise Daddy's gonna get!"

BLACK SHEEP: DEATH TO HERO! DEATH TO HERO! DEATH TO HERO!

LIL' MONSTER: *(to Warrior.)* D'you believe that?

*No response from **Warrior**.*

>Warrior....?

WARRIOR: What would I know? I'm just an idiot.

LIL' MONSTER: *(crestfallen, tearful)* But... why would he wanna do that? He fought for us, he put his life on the line for us? I don't understand. Daddy?

DADDY LOVE: Come to Daddy, come to Daddy.

***Daddy Love** takes her in his arms and comforts her.*

SMOOTHY: Power, of course. He wanted power all to himself. He wanted to be like the scum. You heard him, he was in league with Mr Jones. He was becoming one of 'em. The enemy within.

BLACK SHEEP: ENEMY WITHIN! ENEMY WITHIN! ENEMY WITHIN!

DUCKLIFE: Whass gonna happen to the windmill?

SMOOTHY: Simple. Daddy's wants us to rebuild it.

A collective groan among the animals.

SMOOTHY: Without the windmill, we're lost. We'll starve and the scum will take back the farm. And what do you think they'll do to you if that happens? You think they'll forget everything, pretend the revolution never happened, welcome you back with open arms? No, I'll tell you what they'll do to you. First, they'll string you up, they'll leave you hanging there for days, then they'll come for you in the night with sharp knives in their hands, and they'll slit your throats slowly and let you bleed to death. And the final insult, brothers and sisters? They'll urinate over you and let your carcass be picked apart by birds because to them you are nothing, because to them *you* are the scum!

A shudder runs through the animals.

***Smoothy** turns to **Warrior**.*

>Our favourite son, we're depending on you.

*All the animals turn to **Warrior** expectantly.*

WARRIOR: Gotta work harder!

DADDY LOVE: What must we do, my children?

ALL: GOTTA WORK HARDER! GOTTA WORK HARDER! GOTTA WORK HARDER!

SCENE NINE

It's been a bad harvest. The animals are starving. Their bones are showing through their skins/hides now. They scavenge anywhere for food, often fighting each other for scraps.

GOATFACE: Food, I want food.

DONKEYKICK: Anything, summin'.

PIGEONHEAD: Summin', anything.

DUCKLIFE: Gotta eat.

RED HEN: Gonna starve.

The animals see a rat. They pounce on it.

GOATFACE: A rat!

DONKEYKICK: Grab it!

PIGEONHEAD: Tear it apart!

DUCKLIFE: Rip it to pieces!

RED HEN: Bones an' all!

They tear the rat apart and wolf it down. It is a pathetic, wretched sight.

PIGEONHEAD: Still hungry…

They look around for scraps of food, there is none, they stare murderously at the young animals, their eyes come to rest on one of the youngest, they start to advance towards him/her.

***Daddy Love** and **Smoothy** enter.*

The pack backs away immediately from the young animal.

Smoothy picks up the remains of the rat.

SMOOTHY: First rule of Revolution Farm! What is it?

BLACK SHEEP: All animals are the same!

SMOOTHY: Correct! Well done comrade.

GOATFACE: It was only a rat.

SMOOTHY: Only a rat? What kind of talk is that? A rat is one of us. Are you not one of us? Brothers and sisters, do we need to re-educate you? Or perhaps you are a lost cause already? Perhaps you are... the enemy within... eh brothers and sisters?

BLACK SHEEP: I am not the enemy, Sir! I believe in the Revolution, Sir!

I will kill those who are against us, Sir! I will give up my life for the beautiful cause, Sir!

WARRIOR: Let 'em be. It's been a bad harvest. We ain't eaten for weeks. Everybody's hungry.

A commotion goes up, the animals are starving, end of their tether.
Smoothy motions for quiet.

SMOOTHY: The scum are savages. Let's give 'em what they want. They want blood. We'll give it to 'em. But they'll have to pay!

Daddy Love's *dogs bring in two cocks, and drops them on the floor.*

SMOOTHY: Yes, this is what they want. And this is what we're gonna give 'em! Fight! Fight! Fight!

Smoothy *bullies the animals into joining in.*

ALL: FIGHT! FIGHT! FIGHT!

The two cocks fight each other until one of them is killed. The victorious cock struts around the farm.

COCK: I'm the leader! I'm the leader!

ALL: LEADER! LEADER! LEADER!

LIL' MONSTER: This ain't what Revolution Farm is about!

SMOOTHY: And what would you know?

LIL' MONSTER: I know this ain't right.

SMOOTHY: Who wants the scum back?

He makes a slicing motion across his neck.

It's for the good of us all. Sacrifices have to be made. No one said it'd be easy. The scum'll pay good money for this.

CHICKENS: We'd rather starve!

DADDY LOVE: What have I done to deserve this? I try, I really try to love you, but all the time you reject my love. You'd rather starve? Then

	starve you will. No food for the chickens! Not one grain!
LIL' MONSTER:	You don't have to do this.
SMOOTHY:	Tough decisions, hard choices, Lil' Monster. Never easy to make.
LIL' MONSTER:	Like sleeping in the scum's beds? Like keepin' the milk to yourself? Like changin' the rules? Was they hard choices, Smoothy?
SMOOTHY:	You do have quite a mouth on you.
LIL' MONSTER:	Tell me I'm wrong. Tell me it's not true. Tell me I'm imagining it. But I thought we was all together, all the same, all equal.
SMOOTHY:	You sound just like the traitor Hero. *(spits in disgust)*
LIL' MONSTER:	Good. 'Cos I'll tell you this, I knows you never liked him, but he won us the important battles, I never saw you Smoothy, or you Daddy Love, when it all kicked off. I never saw you once. Where were you? Makin' hard choices 'bout which warm bed to sleep in that day?
SMOOTHY:	O I see, is that what this is all about? Sleeping in the scum's beds. Well, why didn't you say?
LIL' MONSTER:	Beds are what scum sleep in!

SMOOTHY: May I correct you. Beds with sheets are what scum sleep in. We sleep in beds yes, but not with sheets. Sheets are not acceptable. Those are the rules.

LIL' MONSTER: You've changed 'em!

SMOOTHY: Rubbish. We never changed anything. You're imagining it.

LIL' MONSTER: Beds are what scum sleep in. That's what it said, didn't it?

The animals are confused, they can't remember.

Well, didn't it?

*She turns to **Warrior**.*

Warrior, you remember?

WARRIOR: *(embarrassed)* I... I... dunno, Lil'... never read 'em...

SMOOTHY: You struggle a bit with reading don't you, Lil' Monster? I think you've made a mistake. We never changed a thing.

LIL' MONSTER: *(pointing at Daddy Love)* The only mistake we've made is letting him be leader!

***Daddy Love** emits a high pitched scream. the attack dogs pounce on **Lil' Monster**: they drag her down by the neck and maul her. **Warrior** kicks the dogs off **Lil' Monster**, and she escapes. A terrible, vicious fight ensues between **Warrior** and the dogs.*

LIL' MONSTER: Stop 'em! Stop 'em! They'll kill him!

Daddy Love calls off his dogs.

The animals are rigid with shock and fear.

Smoothy looks wildly around him. He knows he's got to contain the situation.

SMOOTHY: Brothers and sisters, last night there was an assassination attempt on our beloved Leader!

Gasps from the animals.

We think it was Hero.

Pause.

We think he's returned to the farm.

Pause.

Some of you have reported sightings of him.

He nods towards Black Sheep.

BLACK SHEEP: He comes mostly in the night... mostly...

The animals peer at each other nervously.

The cock is still strutting and preening, oblivious to the danger building up around him.

COCK: I killed him! I killed him! I killed him!

DADDY LOVE: And would you kill me too, brother?

Daddy Love *takes the cock and cradles it in his arms lovingly.*

> I have so much love in my heart for you. You do not know. You do not know how overwhelming this love is. My heart feels like it's bursting. Come to Daddy. Come to Daddy. Let him hold you. Heal your wounds.
>
> You are angry. Daddy understands. Daddy understands everything. This is what Hero has done to you. He has turned you. O my beloved children beware, the shadow of the traitor. Hero is everywhere. He comes in the night. When we are fast asleep. He steals our food, urinates in our beds, stares at us in the dark. O be careful, my children, Hero is everywhere, he's all around us, watching us, waiting, waiting for his chance. Confess my child, confess to your crimes, and I will heal you, I will love you again, I will be your Father again. Whisper, my child, whisper to me what you have done.

He breaks the cock's neck. He wipes away a tear.

> There are more traitors.

Pause

> He named them.

Pause

> Come forward.

Pause

> I know who you are.

Pause.

> I know your names.

A few animals come forward gingerly. They bow their heads in shame and mutter that 'Hero made me do it'.

> Please, I want to be alone. Daddy is upset. Daddy doesn't want you to see him cry. Close the doors after you.

The animals troop out of the barn.

There are blood curling screams.

SCENE TEN

Winter, classroom. The animals, starving and freezing cold, are peering at the latest amendment to the rules, trying to work out what it says.

GOATFACE: What's it say?

DONKEYKICK: Dunno.

GOATFACE: Hey, Lil'!

Lil' Monster struggles to read the new rule, but after a few attempts, successfully reads it out aloud.

'Killing... each other... is what scum do... 'cept when it's right'

PIGEONHEAD: What's it mean?

LIL' MONSTER: *(wearily)* It means they've changed the rules.

She goes back to Warrior.

BLACK SHEEP: *(munching on a big juicy apple)* Daddy Love knows best.

GOATFACE: That's what you always say.

BLACK SHEEP: You gotta problem wiv that?

Black Sheep rears up on his hind legs and Goatface backs away. strangely, Black Sheep appears to stay upright.

PIGEONHEAD: What's Warrior think?

LIL' MONSTER: Leave him be. He's exhausted.

PIGEONHEAD: Well, what about you?

LIL' MONSTER: *(bitterly)* I think it was always like that. We've made a mistake. Daddy Love knows best. He always knows best. We're nothing but stupid, dumb animals.

***Smoothy** enters throwing money at the animals who grab and claw and gouge each other to get at the notes. He's a little drunk. His hands are blood-stained too.*

SMOOTHY: Good news, glorious heroes of the revolution! Look, we've made a profit. Yes, that's right, grab it, put it under your beds, hide it away, do whatever you want. It's a new beginning, my beautiful children. A brand new beginning. Yes, it's been difficult, tough decisions had to be made, it was painful, hard, oh excruciating at times, (not least for Our Leader), but remember, we're all in this together. All in this together.

*The animals stare blankly at **Smoothy**.*

(triumphantly) Revolution Farm is finally ours!

No reaction.

What, no chants? No cheers? No joyous cries? I'll say it once again. Revolution Farm is ours!

Still no reaction from the animals.

	(viciously) Say it! Say it now! I demand you say it now!
ALL:	*(without conviction)* REVOLUTION FARM IS OURS. REVOLUTION FARM IS OURS. REVOLUTION FARM IS OURS.
PIGEONHEAD:	This ain't real. It's fake
GOATFACE:	What you talking about?
PIGEONHEAD:	It ain't got no picture of the Queen
DONKEYKICK:	Well, who's that then?

They have a closer look

GOATFACE:	It's Mr Jones!
LIL' MONSTER:	*(to **Smoothy**)* You... idiot!!!
SMOOTHY:	The treacherous scum!

The Hens come rushing into the classroom.

RED HEN:	They're attacking the windmill!!!
SMOOTHY:	Warrior! Warrior! Wake up! They're attacking!

Warrior *wakes groggily, he's in no state to fight.*

SMOOTHY:	The windmill's being attacked! Kill 'em Warrior, kill 'em!

Lil' Monster *jumps in.*

LIL' MONSTER: We work as a team. We keep together. When one goes down, another takes his place. The line must be held. You got that?

ALL: WE KEEP TOGETHER!
WE KEEP TOGETHER!
WE KEEP TOGETHER!

Smoothy exits quickly.

SCENE ELEVEN

The animals lie in a heap, bloodied and bandaged, like a scene from the trenches in WW1. They've won the Battle, but at a terrible cost. Many animals have died in the fighting. **Daddy Love** *and* **Smoothy** *celebrate with a bottle of whisky.*

SMOOTHY: Rejoice! Rejoice! Victory is ours!

WARRIOR: They had guns

SMOOTHY: Ha! Guns will not defeat us.

WARRIOR: We lost a lot of soldiers.

SMOOTHY: Just rejoice at that victory… Rejoice! After me everybody –

REJOICE! REJOICE! REJOICE!

ALL: *(half-heartedly)* REJOICE…
REJOICE…
REJOICE…

SMOOTHY: Who said the revolution will not be bloody? Who said it wouldn't inflict terrible casualties on us? Who said it wouldn't stretch us to the very limits of our endurance? But revolutions can never be peaceful. They can never be bloodless. They can never be without sacrifice. Because freedom and justice is never given away easily. No, we have to seize it, kill for it, die for it. And now we have to hold on to it for our lives. Our enemies have hearts

of pure evil and they will stop at nothing
to destroy this beautiful paradise of ours.
Heroes. All of you. Heroes.

***Daddy Love** is weeping.*

No one is convinced by this.

***Smoothy** comforts **DADDY LOVE**. **DL** lets out a high pitched
scream.*

The animals scatter in all directions.

SMOOTHY: O don't run, don't be scared. Daddy is only mourning. Mourning for his beautiful dead children who sacrificed their lives for our great cause. We shall not forget them. We shall never forget them. No, we will remember for ever! Look, medals. Medals for all of you. And whisky to celebrate. Celebrate this wonderful, glorious victory.

GOATFACE: We ain't supposed to drink.

SMOOTHY: Who says?

DONKEYKICK: You.

SMOOTHY: Me? What did I say?

GOATFACE: Alcohol is what scum drink.

SMOOTHY: Well, not quite, my brave warriors. We meant to say alcohol is what scum drink, 'cept when there's good cause to celebrate. And what better cause than the defeat of

> our vicious, cruel enemies. To our brave and noble comrades, they fought like beasts of the jungle, and gave their lives up willingly!

Some of the younger animals start to whimper and wail in distress at losing their loved ones.

> Oh look now, heroes don't cry, do they?

PIGEONHEAD: Daddy's cryin'.

SMOOTHY: That's because he feels responsible.

BLACK SHEEP: The scum is responsible! Kill the scum!

SMOOTHY: *(caressing the sheep)* Thank you, you beautiful creature, so strong, so resolute, so firm... Look, it's not easy being a leader. Sometimes it can be a terrible burden. All that responsibility. And no one to share it with. Think how lonely it must be for Our Great Leader. So stop your crying now, it's not helping anyone.

The animals continue to whimper.

> Stop it! I said stop it! Stop! Stop! Stop!

Lil' Monster *draws the animals close to her and comforts them.*

SMOOTHY: Warrior, the windmill must be rebuilt if we are to complete the revolution.

WARRIOR: You can rely on me.

SMOOTHY: See, Warrior fights another day. Hero of the revolution, I salute you!

He trips over, gets up and totters off. ***Daddy*** *goes too.*

LIL' MONSTER: Warrior, you can say no.

WARRIOR: It's gotta be finished.

LIL' MONSTER: Why?

WARRIOR: 'Cos I said I'd do it. I've given my word. Can't go back on that. What would the soldiers think?

LIL' MONSTER: Go easy, Warrior. Please.

WARRIOR: *(to the animals)* What've we gotta do?

ALL: WORK TILL WE DROP! WORK TILL WE DROP! WORK TILL WE DROP!

The younger animals sit motionless in front of the dead animals, pawing at them, as if they're still alive.

WARRIOR: Alright, take 'em away. Quick. Do it now.

They drag the dead animals away.

SCENE TWELVE

The animals work hard to rebuild the windmill. ***Warrior*** *typically, works harder than ever. But he's lost 30 percent of his body weight and his strength is going. Finally, he collapses.*

DONKEYKICK: Warrior's down! Warrior's down!

Lil' Monster *rushes to* ***Warrior****.*

LIL' MONSTER: Oh Warrior, what did I tell you? Don't overdo it! You silly thing.

She tries to help him up, but it's no good, he can't stand on his own legs now. She is getting worried.

    Get up, I can't do this all by myself.

WARRIOR: I'm done, Lil'.

LIL' MONSTER: Very funny, now get up.

WARRIOR: I can't.

LIL' MONSTER: Yes you can.

WARRIOR: My legs are gone.

LIL' MONSTER: C'mon, here we go.

WARRIOR: Ain't no use.

LIL' MONSTER: Up! Up! Up!

ALL: WARRIOR UP! WARRIOR UP! WARRIOR UP!

Warrior *collapses again.*

LIL' MONSTER: Warrior, if this is a joke.

WARRIOR: Ain't no joke, sweetheart.

GOATFACE: Get Smoothy! Tell him what's happened!

*The animals try to help **Warrior** up.*

***Daddy Love** and **Smoothy** arrive.*

SMOOTHY: O, Warrior, mighty, strong Warrior, what has the scum done to you?

LIL' MONSTER: It ain't the scum, it's your bloody windmill that's done this!

SMOOTHY: We'll take him to hospital straight away, we'll have the best doctors, the most expensive medicines, no expense spared.

LIL' MONSTER: No. He stays with me.

SMOOTHY: Lil' Monster, my dear, look at him, he can't even get up, he needs help, specialist help, we can provide that for him.

LIL' MONSTER: He stays with me. And that's final.

***Smoothy** looks at **Daddy Love**, the animals back away, fearing the worst, but **Daddy Love** simply nods.*

SCENE THIRTEEN

*Night. **Lil' Monster** is nursing **Warrior**. He's in a bad way, but is putting a brave face on it.*

LIL' MONSTER: How is it?

WARRIOR: Right as rain. I think I'll pop out and do a bit more work on the windmill

LIL' MONSTER: Too late. The young'uns have finished it.

WARRIOR: Never!

LIL' MONSTER: Yeah.

WARRIOR: The little rascals!

LIL' MONSTER: You taught 'em well.

WARRIOR: You know what, when I'm better, we'll have a few days off, and we'll just run round the fields, like in the beginning, remember, you know, gentle breeze in our faces, blue skies all around us, we ain't done that for a long time.

LIL' MONSTER: I'd like that.

WARRIOR: Best time I ever had in my life. We was crazy wiv freedom, remember? You sent a couple of sheep flying didn't ya. Knocked 'em in the teeth. Oh but all o' us runnin' free. What a sight. Those were the days eh?

LIL' MONSTER:	Got things to look forward to as well, y'know.
WARRIOR:	Yeah, yeah, course. You alright?
LIL' MONSTER:	Yeah, fine.

Lil' Monster is lost in thought.

WARRIOR:	D'you think I'm stupid?
LIL' MONSTER:	Eh?
WARRIOR:	You think I'm stupid? Be honest.
LIL' MONSTER:	What you talkin' about?
WARRIOR:	What Hero said.
LIL' MONSTER:	Hero wouldn't say that.
WARRIOR:	No, but… am I?
LIL' MONSTER:	What, stupid? Yeah, but you're my stupid, so it don't matter.
WARRIOR:	I walked straight into that.
LIL' MONSTER:	Just a little.

They rubs heads together playfully. ***Warrior*** *sees her books.*

WARRIOR:	Always readin' ain't ya.
LIL' MONSTER:	I enjoy it
WARRIOR:	Don't it hurt?
LIL' MONSTER:	A bit, but it's alright.

WARRIOR: Well, you keep it up.

LIL' MONSTER: Oh I will, don't you worry about that.

SCENE FOURTEEN

Day. The animals are working. Unbeknown to them, a van has arrived and taken **Warrior** *away. The animals look up as it driving away from the farm. They rush to wave goodbye to* **Warrior** *who they can see through the small window at the back of the van.*

DUCKLIFE: Get well Warrior!

RED HEN: See ya!

PIGEONHEAD: Laters!

Lil' Monster pushes herself to the front.

LIL' MONSTER: Can't you read what it says? 'Meatland.' Warrior! Get out! Get out now! They're takin' you to the knacker's yard!

Warrior can be heard trying to kick his way out. But the van speeds away and Warrior is gone.

The animals troop back to their work, disconsolate and confused.

SCENE FIFTEEN

Night. A sombre, downbeat atmosphere hangs over the animals. Nobody is talking. **Smoothy** *enters.*

SMOOTHY: I have some very sad news. Despite the extraordinary care he received and the consummate professionalism of the veterinary surgeons attending him, all paid for at our Great Leader's expense of course, Warrior has died. You might like to know I was at his bed-side during his final hours. I could barely look at him through my tears. A light has gone out today that can never be replaced. And yet... and yet. He wanted me to give you this message: Long live Revolution Farm! Long live Our Great Leader! Those were his very last words.

The animals slowly form a circle around **Smoothy.**

GOATFACE: Why it's say Meatland?

DONKEYKICK: Yeah, on the van, why it's say that?

SMOOTHY: It never said anything of the sort. You must have misread it.

DUCKLIFE: That's what it said.

RED HEN: Yeah, we saw it.

PIGEONHEAD: Everyone saw it.

SMOOTHY: Ridiculous. How would you know? None of you can read.

Lil' Monster comes forward and stands in front of Smoothy. Her expression is one of pure hatred.

LIL' MONSTER: 'Meatland. 100% meat, 100% satisfaction. We take care of hungry stomachs.' I bet they do, eh Smoothy. How's your stomach?

Smoothy is taken aback.

Yeah, I can read now... ain't that a shocker...

SMOOTHY: Well... alright, the truth is it did say that...

The animals start to close in on him.

Wait! Wait! Wait! It's really very simple. The veterinary surgeon bought it off the supermarket and didn't have time to wipe off the old name. Obviously, I can see how this may have confused you, but did you really think Our Great Leader would betray us. How unkind of you. Daddy will be devastated when he hears this.

LIL' MONSTER: You can't even be bothered to lie properly anymore!

She strikes Smoothy hard across the face.

SMOOTHY: You all saw that. She hit me. An unprovoked attack. I've got you now. We'll tear you to pieces. Bit by bit. There'll be nothing left of you when we've finished.

LIL' MONSTER: Why do you hate me so much?

SMOOTHY: Because you're all so ordinary!

LIL' MONSTER: Ordinary? What's wrong with that?

SMOOTHY: I can't stand your lack of hunger. Hunger to escape who you are. Where you came from. Content to sit in the same old shit you've always sat in. What do I want? I want to get ahead. I want the very best things in life. And the very best things in life don't come free. You have to fight for them. And if that means others lose out, so be it. Because at the end of the day, there is no such as thing as Revolution Farm. There is only me. You don't get it do you? No one wants to be animals. We want to be humans. We're all humans nowadays. We want what they have. And what do they have? They have things, nice things, expensive things, you don't have anything. Not a thing. You are scum.

Sounds of barking, growling.

GOATFACE: Run, Lil' Monster! Run! The dogs are comin'!

*The dogs run in, but **Lil' Monster** escapes.*

*__Smoothy__ turns to **Goatface**, who backs away.*

SMOOTHY: Kill the traitor!

*The dogs tear **Goatface** to pieces.*

SCENE SIXTEEN

A year later. **Smoothy** *stands in front of a young group of animals.* **Daddy Love** *sits resplendent in a makeshift throne.*

SMOOTHY: Welcome new soldiers. We welcome you to Revolution Farm. We have nursed you as babies, comforted you, caressed you, cradled you in our arms, showered you with constant tender loving care, all for this moment. Your time has come. Are you ready? Are you willing? Do you not love us? Do you not love Our Great Leader?

ANIMALS: YES WE DO!!!

SMOOTHY: Then repeat after me. Animals are scum.

ANIMALS: ANIMALS ARE SCUM!

SMOOTHY: Man is not scum.

ANIMALS: MAN IS NOT NOT SCUM!

SMOOTHY: Clothes are what we wear

ANIMALS: CLOTHES ARE WHAT WE WEAR!

SMOOTHY: Beds are what we sleep in

ANIMALS: BEDS ARE WHAT WE SLEEP IN!

SMOOTHY: Alcohol is what we drink

ANIMALS: ALCOHOL IS WHAT WE DRINK!

SMOOTHY: Killing each other is what we do

ANIMALS:	KILLING EACH OTHER IS WHAT WE DO!
SMOOTHY:	And finally, brothers and sisters, the most important rule of all. All animals are the same but some are not so same as others!
ANIMALS:	ALL ANIMALS ARE THE SAME BUT SOME ARE NOT SO SAME AS OTHERS!

A hooded figure moves silently and secretly among the crowds, handing out flyers that read: 'everyone link up at the barn tonight 12 sharp, bring ya sticks and clubs, pass it on!' It's Lil' Monster.

THE END.

ABOVE: Kevin Kinson, Katie Arnstein, Andreas Angelis
BELOW: Revolution Farm company

ABOVE: Kevin Kinson, Nicola Alexis, Andreas Angelis
BELOW: Kevin Kinson, Katie Arnstein

Samuel Caseley, Andreas Angelis

Photos courtesy of Prodeepta Das